Triumphs of Life

DOREENA WILSON

Copyright © 2024 Doreena Wilson.

All rights reserved. No part of this book may be reproduced, stored, or transmitted by any means—whether auditory, graphic, mechanical, or electronic—without written permission of both publisher and author, except in the case of brief excerpts used in critical articles and reviews. Unauthorized reproduction of any part of this work is illegal and is punishable by law.

ISBN: 979-8-89419-034-1 (sc)
ISBN: 979-8-89419-035-8 (hc)
ISBN: 979-8-89419-036-5 (e)

Because of the dynamic nature of the Internet, any web addresses or links contained in this book may have changed since publication and may no longer be valid. The views expressed in this work are solely those of the author and do not necessarily reflect the views of the publisher, and the publisher hereby disclaims any responsibility for them.

One Galleria Blvd., Suite 1900, Metairie, LA 70001
(504) 702-6708

CONTENTS

On My Mind 1

Poetic Visions 29

Rainy Days 69

Starry Nights 107

On My Mind

BY
DOREENA WILSON

DEDICATION

I dedicate this book to the people that live in my hometown Milwaukee, Wisconsin. I also dedicate this book to the people in my home state and around the united States for without them I would not have been able to write this book.

FORWARD

I forward this book to you the readers who will buy and read my book of poetry. I thank all of you my readers for taking the time to read my book. Without you my readers out there I would not have anyone except the people that I know to share how well I write poetry.

BEAUTIFUL THINGS

Beautiful Things are on my mind throughout the day. Beautiful Things makes me smile. Beautiful Things is what makes everyone happy. Beautiful Things is a wonderful thing Beautiful Things also makes the world a beautiful place to live.

TEARS

Tears are something that everyone has when someone close to them dies. Tears are something that comes when people are full of joy. Tears are something that babies and little children does when they want something. Tears are something that people do when they are full of pain. Tears are also something that people do when things do not go right.

RAINY DAY PEOPLE

Rainy Day People makes me feel like I do not have to feel afraid. Rainy Day People always reminds me that I am not alone when I feel depressed. Rainy Day People does not mind if I cry a little bit. Rainy Day People seems like they do not have a care in the world.

GOING BANANAS

Going Bananas is what I think today's society is turning out to be. Going Bananas is something that I feel like most people in our world minds are going. Going Bananas seems like to me to be the new normal.

BASKET CASES

Basket Cases is something that I feel is how I see our world today. Basket Cases is something that I think today's world is getting into. Basket Cases is also something I feel that our world will never come out of.

ABSENTEEISM

Absenteeism is something that happens in cases that is unexpected. Absenteeism is also something that happens a lot. Absenteeism is something that happens because of an illness. Absenteeism is something that happens because something else comes up.

CHRISTMAS CAROLING

Christmas Caroling is something that a group of people come together and sing. Christmas Caroling is when carolers come out at Christmas time. Christmas Caroling is also something that is a yearly tradition at he end of every year. Christmas Caroling is something that is fun to do.

RAGGEDY ANN AND ANDY

Raggedy Ann And Andy are two famous dolls that children like to play with. Raggedy Ann And Andy are two beautiful early American dolls that is a part of the American tradition and history. Raggedy Ann And Andy is over a century old.

COLORFUL PRINTS

Colorful Prints are so beautiful to look at. Colorful Prints comes in many different prints. Colorful Prints in many different styles. Colorful Prints comes in many different designs. Colorful Prints comes on many different fabrics. Colorful Prints comes in many different colors.

A BIG BRIGHT STAR

A Big Bright Star is what led the three wise men to the town of David. A Big Bright Star was different from any other star. A Big Bright Star had light that was brighter than any other star.

A BOUQUET OF FLOWERS

A Bouquet Of Flowers is something that makes my day. A Bouquet Of Flowers is something that can brighten anyone's day. A Bouquet Of Flowers is also something that smells so wonderful. A Bouquet Of Flowers is something that is beautiful.

SHINNING LIKE DIAMONDS

Shinning Like Diamonds is what your eyes do to me. Shinning Like Diamonds is how the light shines in the the black of night. Shinning Like Diamonds is a bright lamp that shines through the clouds on a cloudy day. Shinning Like Diamonds is what I want my life to shine like.

THE SCHOLAR

The Scholar is someone everyone looks up to for advice for all kinds of subjects. The Scholar is someone who is knowledgeable about all kinds of topics. The Scholar is a person who has several PhD's in different majors. The Scholar is well educated.

THE JUKEBOX

The Jukebox is something that is well gone into the past. The Jukebox is something that we do not see anymore. The Jukebox had all of the top 40 hits on it. The Jukebox had a sound to it that was not like your record player at home. The Jukebox was something that we saw all of the bars and restaurants.

INTO THE NIGHT

Into The Night is where the night owls go into until the dawn comes. Into The Night where the party people go into until the sun rises. Into The Night the time when most people are a sleep until day comes.

THE CLASSES

The Classes comes in hundreds of categories. The Classes comes in so many different subjects. The Classes sometimes conflicts with each other. The Classes are all over the world. The Classes can connect with each other. The Classes are endless.

THE BEER GARDEN

The Beer Garden is a place where a lot of people can get together and enjoy an ice cold mug of frosty beer. The Beer Garden canes around every year when the whether gets warm. The Beer Garden is always in a large park where big crowds of people come together and have a good time.

CHEERS TO YOU

Cheers To You for all of your accomplishments. Cheers To You for all of your success. Cheers To You for you new job that you have got hired. Cheers To You for all other great things that you are going to achieve. Cheers To You for being you.

THUMBS UP

Thumbs Up for a wonderful job. Thumbs Up to the future. Thumbs Up for your continued support. Thumbs Up for saving the day. Thumbs Up for great team work. Thumbs Up for our long term friendship.

BEHIND THE DOOR

Behind The Door there is a big party. Behind The Door there is a lot of music. Behind The Door there is a lot cheering. Behind The Door there a lot of food and drinks being served. Behind The Door there is a lot of happy people.

THE THRILL OF IT ALL

The Thrill Of It All was when I met you. The Thrill Of It All was when we had dinner together. The Thrill Of It All is when we have long talks. The Thrill Of It All is because we have been together for over 24 years. The Thrill Of It All is that we will always be together.

REFLECTIONS

Reflections is something that I have at the end of a busy day. Reflections is when I reflect on the events that was fun. Reflections is when I reflect on something that was successful. Reflections is something that I reflect on that was positive.

THE HORSE RACES

The Horse Races is a sport that I enjoy watching on TV. The Horse Races is so exciting to watch. The Horse Races is a sport that is loved by many people all over the world. The Horse Races is a sport that has be around for over a century.

THE CHEST

The Chest is a place where I keep a lot of my personal belongings. The Chest is a beautiful piece of furniture that is made of dark mahogany wood. The Chest has only two drawers in it. The Chest has been in my possession for over 20 years.

SPORTS FANATICS

Sports Fanatics are a lot of fun to be around. Sports Fanatics knows a lot about many different kinds of sports. Sports Fanatics can teach you a lot about many different sports. Sports Fanatics always get excited about sports. Sports Fanatics comes from all different kinds of walks of life.

THE DOLL HOUSE

The Doll House is something that I have had every since I was five-years-old. The Doll House is something I used play with when I was a little girl. The Doll House is made of wood. The Doll House was painted red and green. The Doll House is older than I am.

TALK SHOW HOSTS

Talk Show Hosts are all over the radio and TV. Talk Show Hosts talks about many different topics. Talk Show Hosts can be funny. Talk Show Hosts can be entertaining. Talk Show Hosts can be celebrities. Talk Show Hosts can be former athletes.

THE CLASS REUNIONS

The Class Reunions was a lot of fun. The Class Reunions is where I got to see a lot of my old classmates. The Class Reunions had a lot of food and drinks. The Class Reunions music and dancing. The Class Reunions had some of my old teachers.

DREAMS

Dreams comes in many different forms. Dreams can be a nightmare. Dreams can be funny. Dreams can be romantic. Dreams can visions for the future. Dreams can be sometimes remembered. Dreams can be sometimes forgotten. Dreams can good. Dreams can be bad. Dreams are always a part of our lives.

TEDDY BEARS

Teddy Bears comes in many different colors. Teddy Bears comes in many different styles. Teddy Bears are for people of all ages. Teddy Bears always has a smile on them. Teddy Bears brings many smiles to many different people all over the world.

THE CHEF

The Chef is the one person who can prepare exquisite dishes. The Chef wears a white double breasted tunic with a big white hat. The Chef is always looking for new ways to prepare a dish. The Chef is always asking for feedback on her dishes.

YEARS GONE BYE

Years Gone Bye always have fond memories about them. Years Gone Bye has gone bye so fast. Years Gone Bye always leave behind thoughts that were good. Years Gone Bye always leave behind thoughts that were bad. Years Gone Bye will never be forgotten.

PUBLIC SPEAKING

Public Speaking is something that I enjoy doing because I always have something to say. Public Speaking is a lot of fun. Public Speaking takes a lot of thought. Public Speaking takes a lot of time to research and prepare. Public Speaking takes practice.

STRAIGHT TO THE TOP

Straight To The Top is where I am heading. Straight To The Top is where a lot of people are heading. Straight To The Top takes a lot of hare work. Straight To The Top is how I got noticed. Straight To The Top can make you feel great about yourself.

THE TEA CUP

The Tea Cup is what I always use to drink my tea. The Tea Cup is always there for me when I want a cup of tea. The Tea Cup has a lot of beautiful designs on it. The Cup holds a lot of tea. The Tea Cup is easy to keep clean.

THE SUGAR BOWL

The Sugar Bowl is a good dish for me to put my sugar. The Sugar Bowl has a matching lid to cover it. The Sugar Bowl never gets broken. The Sugar Bowl always looks nice sitting on my counter top.

SALT AND PEPPER

Salt And Pepper is something that gives a lot of flavor to my food. Salt And Pepper goes together like a hand in glove. Salt And Pepper are two spices that have been around for many centuries. Salt And Pepper is very easy to use on your favorite dishes.

FAMOUS PEOPLE

Famous People has always been around. Famous People is someone who everyone looks up to as roll models. Famous People is someone who everyone always gets excited about. Famous People are extraordinary. Famous People have a God given talent.

THE KITCHEN CUPBOARD

The Kitchen Cupboard has a lot of space to all of my dishes. The Kitchen Cupboard has a lot of space to put all of my pots, pans and skillets. The Kitchen Cupboards are is beautiful to look at.

THE BOOK SHELF

The Book Shelf is some thing that I put all of my videos and CD's on. The Book Shelf is something that I put my collectibles on. The Book Shelf is made of wood. The Book Shelf sits in my living room. The Book Shelf stand next to my TV stand.

AWARDS AND CERTIFICATES

Awards And Certificates is something that I have a lot of. Awards And Certificates is something that I have received a lot of for my volunteer work. Awards And Certificates is something that I have received for my fine accomplishments. Awards And Certificates is something that I have received for finishing short classes.

THE TELEPHONE

The Telephone was an excellent invention. The Telephone makes life so much easier to communicate with other people. The Telephone is something we all take for granted. The Telephone is something we all cannot do without. The Telephone is something is here to stay.

PICTURES

Pictures is something that everyone loves. Pictures has been around for more than a century. Pictures say words that cannot be said. Pictures can be in color. Pictures can be in black and white. Pictures are something we cannot live without.

THE STAMP COLLECTION

The Stamp Collection is something that I have a lot of. The Stamp Collection is something that I will have forever. The Stamp Collection is something I have collected over the years. The Stamp Collection something that a lot of people have. The Stamp Collection that I have is over 200 stamps.

CHRISTIAN MUSIC

Christian Music is something that I love. Christian Music that I always listen to. Christian Music is something that I always enjoy singing along with. Christian Music is something that I listen throughout the day. Christian Music is something that listen to in the morning. Christian Music is something that I listen to a night. Christian Music will always be a part of life.

WHEN I PRAY

When I Pray I thank God for all of my blessings. When I Pray I pray for all of our troops around the world and the one who are serving right her in the US. When I Pray I pray I pray all of our government officials who are elected to federal, state and local offices.

MY BEDROOM

My Bedroom is the one place that I consider to be my private place. My Bedroom is not only where I sleep and get dressed. My Bedroom is where I keep all of my clothes and belongings. My Bedroom is do all of my thinking about what I have planned for each day of the week. My Bedroom is where I have my quiet time with the Lord.

MOTHER NATURE

Mother Nature is a force that can be furious. Mother Nature can be wonderful. Mother Nature is God's beautiful creation. Mother Nature can work with us. Mother Nature Mother Nature is something that we cannot do without. Mother Nature will always be a part of our lives.

ROSES

Roses are very beautiful. Roses smells wonderful. Roses in many colors. Roses have thorns on them. Roses is something everyone loves. Roses is a flower that needs a lot of care. Roses grow in gardens where someone with a green thumb who knows how to grow them.

THE LETTER

The Letter is something that I received from my friend. The Letter was something that I received unexpectedly. The Letter wished me goodwill and good health. The Letter made me fill very good. The Letter was from my friend Caroline.

THE BIRD CAGE

The Bird Cage was something that I loved to look at. The Bird Cage had two parakeets in it. The Bird Cage was a lot of work to keep clean. The Bird Cage was something that I became attached to. The Bird Cage was beautiful.

THE CHAIRMAN

The Chairman was very helpful to our organization. The Chairman had a lot of great ideas. The Chairman knew exactly what steps to take. The Chairman was well qualified The Chairman had a since of humor.

THE CHAIR

The Chair is very comfortable to sit in. The Chair has a lot of room to sit and relax. The Chair is made of a forest green corduroy material. The Chair sits in my living room. The Chair is place where my guests loves to sit when they come to visit.

THE GLASS DOLL

The Glass Doll is very shinny and beautiful. The Glass Doll something that I have had for many years. The Glass Doll looks like it is real. The Glass Doll was well made. The Glass Doll is a piece of collection that anyone would love to have.

THE VEGETABLE GARDEN

The Vegetable Garden is filled with all kinds of veggies. The Vegetable Garden was well kept. The Vegetable Garden is something that would make a real gardener happy. The Vegetable Garden looks like it is ready to be picked.

DAY BY DAY

Day By Day I am very busy. Day By Day seems like they go bye in a split second. Day By Day turns into weeks. Day By Day turns into months. Day By Day turns into years. Day By Day turns into decades. Day By Day goes by very fast.

MY DOLL COLLECTION

My Doll Collection is a very big collection. My Doll Collection was an expensive collection. My Doll Collection makes all of my collections complete. My Doll Collection has a personality that is all its own. My Doll Collection will be in my collection for many years to come.

DINNER TIME

Dinner Time is my favorite time of the day. Dinner Time is a time when I enjoy cooking my favorite recipes. Dinner Time a time that everyone loves. Dinner Time is a time that I look forwards to planning my meals.

CHURCH

Church is the one place where I love to attend. Church an important part a Christians life. Church has a lot of praise and worship. Church has a lot of testimony. Church has a lot of preaching.

VETERANS DAY

Veterans Day is a very important day. Veterans Day is a day that is set aside to honor both our fallen heroes and our vets. Veterans Day is a day when we come together every year to thank our heroes for their sacrifice and service. Veterans Day is day that is set aside to watch the memorial services. Veterans Day is a day that is set aside to enjoy watching our veterans day parades.

ABOUT THE AUTHOR

In my book titled Triumphs of Life I decided to write about the things that God has helped me to triumph over in my life. I had a lot of things to think about with the writing of this book. It did not take me as long to write this book because everything that I thought about came to me very easily. I had a little bit of writers block with the titles of the poems for this book however I had no idea of what to say.

The things that I wrote about in this book were things that is a part of my everyday life. I had a lot of fun writing this book because this was not my first time of writing poetry. I enjoy writing poetry very much and I hope that my readers will find that I have put forth a lot thought into my writing. I always get a lot of feedback about my writing and how well written my poems are.

I hope that you my readers will agree with me about the writing of my poems and that I did my best to write about the things that other people can relate to. I will try to continue to write poetry as long as I have the ideas that come to my mind and my everyday life.

Poetic Visions

BY
DOREENA WILSON

DEDICATION

I dedicate this book to the everyday hardships and joys in our lives. I also dedicate this book to God for without him being in my life I would not have even been able to come up with all of the wonderful things that I have written in this book.

FORWARD

I forward this book to God first and foremost who gives me the everyday strength and mind to do and write the things that I am able to do and write about everyday.

MY VISIONS FOR THE FUTURE

My Visions For The Future is that everyone no matter what age group you are in you can still make a difference in our troubled world. My Visions For The Future is that no matter what educational background or educational level you are in you can still make a difference in our troubled world. My Visions For The Future is that no matter what ethnic, race or sex you are you can still make a difference in our troubled world. My Visions For The Future is that if you are already doing something to make a difference you have already begun the healing process.

OUR VETERANS THAT HAS PAID THE ULTIMATE PRICE

Our Veterans That Has Paid The Ultimate Price have already done a great job to defend our great country. Our Veterans That Has Paid The Ultimate Price have my unending respect and love for them. Our Veterans That Has Paid The Ultimate Price deserve everything that our great country can give them for their service and bravery. Our Veterans That Has Paid The Ultimate Price will never be forgotten by our fellow American citizens.

WHY WE SHOULD ALWAYS REMEMBER OUR FALLEN POLICE OFFICERS

Why We Should Always Remember Our Fallen Police Officers is because they are our heroes. Why We Should Always Remember Our Fallen Police Officers is because they always put their lives on the line for everyone in their communities. Why We Should Always Remember Our Fallen Police Officers is because they put the all into everything they do for us. Why We Should Always Remember Our Fallen Police Officers is because they deserve our utmost never ending respect and salutes for their never ending service.

MY NEVER ENDING TALENT TO WRITE POETRY

My Never Ending Talent To Write Poetry is endless because I have a lot of different topics to write about. My Never Ending Talent To Write Poetry is because of one of my former instructors at Milwaukee Area Technical College Mrs. Mary Louise Stebbins encouraging our class to write poetry. My Never Ending Talent To Write Poetry is also because of the encouragement of my former instructor I had a big urgency to get started writing as soon as possible.

MY ABLILTY TO HELP OTHERS

My Ability To Help Others takes a lot of know how and brainstorming. My Ability To Help Others is not just for my gratification but to honor God. My Ability To Help Others comes from the goodness of my heart. My Ability To Help Others is because when I see someone in need of some help I am always ready to reach out to ask them for their permission to see if I can be of some service to them.

I HAVE A LOVE TO SERVE GOD

I Have A Love To Serve God because he has blessed me with all of the blessings that he can give me. I Have A Love To Serve God because of his undying love and grace for me. I Have A Love To Serve God because of the many people that have helped me with my recovery from my mental illness and physical problems over the years. I Have A Love To Serve God because of all of the wonderful professionals and family members that has come to my aide I now have excellent health and a sound mind to reach out and serve God.

EDUCATORS MAKES A DIFFERENCE

Educators Makes A Difference because they took the time and energy to go out to get a higher education to become educators to teach. Educators Makes A Difference because they work hard and long hours to make sure that the students that teach get a good academic background. Educators Makes A Difference because the will go out of their way to teach you and help in different ways that they know that can help you to learn. Educators Makes A Difference because they know that in the end everything that they do will work out in the end.

I KNOW THAT JESUS IS COMING BACK

I know That Jesus Is Coming Back because this is what he promised in the bible. I Know That Jesus Is Coming Back because of all of the sin and problems that we have in this world. I Know That Jesus Is Coming Back because he said that it will get worst before it gets better. I Know That Jesus Is Coming Back because of all of the prophecies that are being fulfilled. I Know That Jesus Is Coming Back because of all of the wars that have been taking place for almost over the past 20 years. I Know That Jesus Is Coming Back because everything he said that would happen is happening.

I LIKE TO SIT AND LISTEN

I Like To Sit And Listen because it gives me a clear understanding about what other people think and what they have to say. I Like To Sit And Listen because it makes me think clearer about what I have learned and experienced in my life. I Like To Sit And Listen to what other people for different educational backgrounds and walks of life have to say. I Like To Sit And Listen because I can always learn something new and exciting.

I HAVE A BETTER UNDERSTANDING ABOUT HOW TO HANDLE A CRISIS

I Have A Better Understanding About How To Handle A Crisis because of all of the psychiatry appointments, group therapy and assertiveness training sessions that I have had in my life. I Have A Better Understanding About How To Handle A Crisis because I wanted all of the professional help that I could get to overcome what was wrong in my life. I Have A Better Understanding About How To Handle A Crisis because I knew that if I did not get the help that I needed it would be very hard for me to recover and make a good life for myself and help other people in some of the same situations I was in.

I WILL NEVER FORGET HOW FAR I HAVE COME

I Will Never Forget How Far I Have Come because I know that God has brought me through thick and thin. I Will Never Forget How Far I Have Come because of all of the wonderful and great accomplishments I have done in my life. I Will Never Forget How Far I Have Come because of all of different people places and things I have seen. I Will Never Forget How Far I Have Come because there is still a lot for me to accomplish in my life.

I HAVE A LOT OF DIFFERENT FRIENDS IN MY LIFE

I Have A Lot Of Different Friends In My Life because I have a love for people. I Have A Lot Of Different Friends In My Life because I am a very friendly person. I Have A Lot Of Different Friends In My Life because I to meet and talk to different people from different walks of life. I Have A Lot Of Different Friends In My Life because I think that making friends is better than making enemies.

THE POWER OF PRAYER

The Power Of Prayer allows me to pray about things that are going wrong in my life rather than getting angry. The Power Of Prayer is a great thing to do because the word of God requires that we must pray on a daily basis. The Power Of Prayer is a must if we want to continue to walk with God. The Power Of Prayer is a powerful thing. The Power Of Prayer keeps close to God. The Power Of Prayer is nothing to take lightly. The Power Of Prayer keeps us strong in the Lord. The Power Of Prayer keeps the enemy away.

LISTENING TO MUSIC

Listening To Music allows me to sit and relax and remember the good old days. Listening To Music is something I like to do because I like to listen to the music of my youth. Listening To Music allows me to go back to those days when the times were simpler. Listening To Music is something that I think that a lot of people like to do. Listening To Music is something that calms me down when I have some free time. Listening To Music is wonderful because there are a lot of beautiful music that I grew up listening to when I was younger.

MY FAVORITE ARTWORK

My Favorite Artwork is the classical color, black and white and abstract art that we all have seen in the art museums. My Favorite Artwork is the kind of Artwork that the classical European artists have drawn and painted. My Favorite Artwork is also the sculpted and pottery artwork. My Favorite Artwork is something that everyone can relate to. My Favorite Artwork is for people of all ages and backgrounds.

I LIKE TO GO SHOPPING

I Like To Go Shopping for myself family and friends. I Like To Go Shopping for anything that is on sale at department stores. I Like To Go Shopping mostly for clothes and toys for my nephew. I Like To Go Shopping for the best deals that I can find. I Like To Go Shopping especially for the holidays weddings and birthdays. I Like To Go Shopping for the things that I know that I would like for myself. I Like To Go Shopping for the essentials. I Like To Go Shopping for T-shirts, jeans, pants, dresses, londere and shoes. I Like To Go Shopping to buy presents to make other people happy.

IT IS TIME FOR PEACE

It Is Time For Peace and healing to come into our world. It Is time For Peace to come and bring an end to the war around the world. It Is Time For Peace to come and bring all of the people in our world back to Christ. It Is Time For Peace to come because know that Jesus is coming back. It Is Time For Peace to come and let everyone know that the end is near. It Is Time For Peace to come and let everyone know that God is watching our every move.

WHERE COULD I GO

Where Could I Go but straight to the Lord. Where Could I Go but to just surrender all. Where Could I Go except to let Jesus know that I love him. Where Could I Go except but to the house of the Lord. Where Could I Go to tell God all of my troubles except but just go on my knees. Where Could I Go but straight to the cross.

KEEP ON THE SUNNY SIDE

Keep On The Sunny Side but only in the sun light. Keep On The Sunny Side right by Jesus. Keep On The Sunny Side but giving the Lord all of the praise glory and honor. Keep On The Sunny Side but thanking God for your blessings. Keep On The Sunny Side right by God letting him know that you love him. Keep On The Sunny Side to let the Lord know that you will never forsake him.

I TRULY BELIEVE

I Truly Believe that the Lord has a plan for all of us. I Truly Believe that God is really love. I Truly Believe that I will never give up on myself. I Truly Believe that I we are all here to glorify God. I Truly Believe that God is working in my life. I Truly Believe that the Lord is really giving me the words to write poetry. I Truly Believe that God has always and always will be with us all until the end.

A LOT TO BE THANKFUL FOR

A lot To Be Thankful For is something that we all have because we are living. A Lot To Be Thankful For is something we all have because Jesus came and died for our sins. A Lot To Be Thankful For is something that I have because I have excellent health a sound mind and salvation. A Lot To Be Thankful For is something we have as Americans a chance to receive a good education graduate get a good job and receive excellent finances and benefits. A Lot To Be Thankful For in this country is that we all have the freedom of free speech.

MY CHANCES OF GETTING A GOOD PAYING JOB

My Chances Of Getting A Good Paying Job is excellent because have a good educational background and good work experiences. My Chances Of Getting A Good Paying Job is wonderful because I am a people person. My Chances Of Getting A Good Paying Job is great because I have a clean record. My Chances Of Getting A Good Paying Job is awesome because I have excellent references. My Chances Of Getting A Good Paying Job is because my former employers all liked me and my performance on my last job. My Chances Of Getting A Good Paying Job will be because I have the ability to please others.

WHAT I HAVE DONE TO HELP OUR VETS

What I Have Done To Help Our Vets is that I have volunteered at the VA hospital. What I Have Done To Help Our Vets by working to volunteer in the Veterans Canteen Cafe Services. What I Have Done To Help Our Vets is that I have donated money to the Veterans of Foreign Wars. What I Have Done To Help Our Vets is that I have helped the disabled vets take their lunch trays to their tables. What I Have Done For Our Vets is that I have prayed for them.

I LIKE TO KEEP UP WITH THE NEWS

I Like To Keep Up With The News because I like to know what is going on around us. I Like To Keep Up With The News because I like to know what is going on locally. I Like To Keep Up With The News because I like to know what is going on in our nation. I Like To Keep Up With The News because I like To know what is going on in our world. I Like To Keep Up With The News is because I like to all about the good news as well as the bad. I Like To Keep Up With The News because I like to be educated.

THE CHARITIES THAT I HAVE HELPED

The Charities That I Have Helped is the kind of charities that supports our vets. The Charities That I Have Helped supports children youth and adult with muscular diseases. The Charities That I Have Helped supports the homeless and the community. The Charities That I Have Helped supports people from all ethnic and walks of life. The Charities That I Have Helped supports christian missionaries around the world and across the nation.

WE ALL BELONG HERE

We All Belong Here because no one is on earth for no reason. We All Belong Here because I believe that God has a purpose for all of us. We All Belong Here because God does not do anything in vein. We All Belong Here because I believe that everyone here has the same rights and we are Gods creatures. We All Belong Here because I Believe that we are all here to glorify God. We All Belong Here because I believe that no one should be cast out. We All Belong Here because I believe that we all have something to offer to one another.

I HAVE MY OWN IDEAS

I Have My Own Ideas about what I believe is wrong with our world. I Have My Own Ideas about what is wrong because the bible says that all have sinned and come short of the glory of God. I Have My Own Ideas because I believe that no one wants to listen to one another. I Have My Own Ideas because I believe that the bible is right about the end of the world.

AS TIME GOES ON

As Time Goes On we all will get old if we live long enough. As Time Goes On I believe that man will eventually destroy himself and that earth. As Time Goes On I think that God is waiting to make sure that his believers will be ready to spend eternity with Jesus. As Time Goes On I believe that Jesus will come as a thief in the night. As Time Goes On I believe that everything that the word of God says is true.

PASSING THE TIME AWAY

Passing The Time Away is something I do by either reading the bible praying or writing poetry. Passing The Time Away is not something I always have time to do because I always have a bessie schedule. Passing The Time Away is not something that I recommend for everyone to do. Passing The Time Away gives me the time to just listen to what God is trying to tell me.

MY FRIENDS

My Friends all comes from different races, ethnic and educational backgrounds. My Friends have different beliefs about who they think God is. My Friends I believe that my friends have a right to believe whatever they want. My Friends and I have a lot in common. My Friends and I have a lot of different thing about us. My Friends and I sometimes have disagreements and we always work it out. My Friends and I like each other a lot. My Friends and I were all raised differently. My Friends and I have total respect for each other.

FIRST

First is the only thing that comes before everything else in life. First is the one thing that we have to do before we can do the second third and so forth. First is the most important thing that we all are taught to do when we have something to do in our busy schedules everyday. First is the only thing that we start out with before we can anything done with what ever we planned to do in out every lives.

SEEMS LIKE

Seems Like everything in our world is just coming apart for many people. Seems Like every time I turn on the news on TV there some kind of tragedy that has taken place. Seems Like some times there is good news and sad news about some body doing something good or bad in their lives. Seems Like practically everybody has lost their minds. Seems Like all of the madness that is going on in our world is never ending. Seems Like some times there is good times and those are the ones that everybody wants to remember.

DISAPPOINTMENT

Disappointment is something that all of us is faced with in our lives when things do not go right. Disappointment is sometimes embarrassing for us. Disappointment is something that can be expected some times. Disappointment is something that we all have no control over. Disappointment can be funny sometimes. Disappointment can make people angry some times. Disappointment is a part of everyday life.

MEMORIES

Memories is all we have left when a friend or family member dies. Memories can some times be funny. Memories can some times be sad. Memories can some times be frustrating. Memories can some times make us angry. Memories can some time leave us wondering. Memories can make us remember all of the things that make us who we are in life.

DILEMMA

Dilemma is something that is a part of life just as so many other things that we deal with everyday. Dilemma is something that makes us think hard about what to do. Dilemma is something that some times comes at the last minute when something has be done. Dilemma is not something that we should take lightly. Dilemma is something that can some times be out of or control. Dilemma is something that can be avoided by planning ahead so that we will not have to face a dilemma.

COLLECTION

Collection is something that all of us have to do when we have business to take of in our everyday lives. Collection is something we all do fall out of our luck and then get back up and collect ourselves. Collection is something that I am always throughout the day when I get telemarketer phone calls from people who want to get my personal information and money. Collection is something that I am always doing 24/7 365 days a year looking out for myself making sure that there is no one trying to give me any problems.

NURSERY SCHOOLS

Nursery Schools is something that did not come out until the early 1970's a time when the early childhood education industry was starting out. Nursery Schools have all come a long way since they started out and they still have a long way to go. Nursery Schools have had problems over the past 50 years or so but they are working on improving them. Nursery Schools is supposed to be a safe haven for young toddlers who are starting out with the educational learning. Nursery Schools have a lot to offer children and young parents.

LACK OF KNOWLEDGE

Lack Of Knowledge is something all us have in one area of life or another. Lack Of Knowledge can be in any subject the we choose ranging in any subject from accounting to zoology. Lack Of Knowledge is something that we have because everyone does not know everything. Lack Of Knowledge is something that I myself is faced with from time to time in my everyday life.

CURIOSITY

Curiosity is something that all of have no matter what age group we are in. Curiosity is not just for young children. Curiosity is something I know that I am faced with every time someone asks me a question about something that I do not know anything about. Curiosity makes us to go look up things a lot of things on the internet. Curiosity makes to want to call up a friend of family member and ask them questions. Curiosity makes us to want to take up a class about something that we might want learn about. Curiosity is something that we all have in our everyday lives.

CONFIDENCE

Confidence is something that I have a lot in myself now that I am older. Confidence is something that everyone does not have in themselves. Confidence is something that I know I have because I have had a good up bringing and I have faith in God. Confidence is something that I had to struggle with when I was in was in and after high school. Confidence is something that I had a lot of help growing into from my church up bringing and from my psychiatrists and therapists. Confidence is something that took a lot of work for me to achieve all of my goals and get my AAS and BS degrees from Milwaukee Area Technical College and the University of Wisconsin-Milwaukee.

ASKING

Asking is something that we all do when we do not know something or when we do not understand something. Asking is something that is sometimes welcomed and sometimes not. Asking is something that comes with educational goals and achievements. Asking is something that I am always doing when I want to know or understand something. Asking is just a part of everyday life.

HUSH

Hush means that we should be quiet if we want to learn or understand something that is vital and important. Hush is something that required sometimes if we want to surprise someone. Hush is something that comes in the night and sometimes in the day. Hush is something that is required if we want to know if something good or bad is going to happen. Hush is vital in our lives.

QUALITY

Quality is something that I take pride in everything I do. Quality is required in all of our business practices. Quality is the most important thing in every ones life. Quality is not the only thing that is required in everyday living but it is required for the finished product. Quality is always required when we put our best foot forward.

POWER

Power is something that our Lord and Savior Jesus Christ has in his presuse blood when he died on the cross for our sins. Power is something that can never go away. Power is something that the Lord have always had. Power is something that he has to heal the sick. Power is something that he has when he wants to stop war and strife. Power is something that he will never cease having.

NOTHINGNESS

Nothingness is something that we all feel at one time or another in our lives. Nothingness is something that we will is a part of our lives when we feel kind of down and depressed. Nothingness is something that we all feel we feel like we do not know what else to do. Nothingness is something that is a part of our part us when we do not feel normal.

SOUNDS

Sounds are something is heard everyday in the big city life. Sounds can be noisy music. Sounds can be the loud sounds of busty traffic. Sounds can be the noise of construction work going on. Sounds can be the crowds of people talking and yelling. Sounds can be the loud voices of children near by. Sounds can be anything that is loud and noisy.

TRIPS

Trips is something that everyone likes to take when they go on vacation. Trips are a lot of fun because I like see all of the beautiful and wonderful seeneries. Trips can be a bother when you have to run errands everyday of the week to take care of everyday life matters. Trips are always something that I look forwards to when I plan a trip or outing to an special event. Trips are always fun when I have a dinner to attend at a restaurant, a wedding a birthday party or a retirement party.

IDEAS

Ideas are something that I have a lot of in my mind when I have something to write about in my poems. Ideas are something that just come to my mind when I am doing something or when I am sleeping at night. Ideas are just something that I believe God has given me. Ideas are something I notice that not everyone has like I have. Ideas just comes naturally for me it is a gift that I have.

COMBINATION

Combination can be something that is several things at one time. Combination can be a combination of a locker. Combination can be anything that has several parts to it. Combination can be anything that requires us to do jobs that needs us to multitask. Combination can be many things at one time.

THOUGHT

Thought can be anything I put my mind to do. Thought takes a lot out of me when I have a big and challenging task to do at hand. Thought is something that I always put towards anything that comes my way. Thought is takes a lot of brainstorming. Thought takes a lot out of me sometimes. Thought sometime comes naturally for me because of all of my real life experiences.

COPY

Copy is something I do when I am instructed to do so. Copy is something you never do when you are taking a test quiz or exam. Copy is something that a lot of people have been accused of in the past. Copy is something that can be done when you are trying learn something. Copy is not something you do when someone else has come up with their own unique ideas.

OVERCOMING

Overcoming is something that I myself have done a lot of in my life time. Overcoming is something that I will continue to throughout the rest of my life. Overcoming is something that I am doing as a christian woman. Overcoming is something that the Lord has helped with all throughout my walk with him.

EVERYONE

Everyone on earth has their own unique qualities. Everyone on earth has their own talents. Everyone on earth has their own beliefs. Everyone on earth has their own ways of handling tragedies in their lives. Everyone on earth has their own ways of handling their own good times in their lives. Everyone on earth has their own ways of celebrating their accomplishments in their lives. Everyone on earth has their own ways of doing things in their lives. Everyone on earth just their own ways of how they want to live their lives.

COMBINE

Combine is something we do when we are trying to get something done at one time. Combine is something we do when we are cooking a recipe in the kitchen. Combine is something we do when we are baking a pastry dish. Combine is something we do when we with a group of other people. Combine is something we also do when we are performing in the fine arts. Combine is something we do when we are playing in a sport activity.

FAVORITES

Favorites is something that we all have in our lives. Favorites can be music. Favorites can be the movies. Favorites can be a dance. Favorites can be the fine arts. Favorites can be a verse in the bible. Favorites can be a toy. Favorites can be a game. Favorites can be a TV show. Favorites can be a recipe or menu. Favorites can be anything that you have had or seen in your life.

THINKING

Thinking is something I do a lot of everyday and night when I know I have something to do whether it is important or not. Thinking is something I know that a lot of people do not always do. Thinking takes a lot of brainstorming really putting forth a lot of thought about what I have to do everyday. Thinking sometimes allows me to ask other people and professionals about what I need to do next. Thinking takes a lot of work for sometimes when I have a deadline to meet in order to get something done on time. Thinking is a very good thing and it pays off in the end.

PLEASING

Pleasing is something that I always seek to do in order to serve God. Pleasing is something that I always seek to do when I put my best foot forward. Pleasing is something that I always get joy in doing for other people. Pleasing is something I do when I work on a job or when I do a volunteer job. Pleasing is something that gives me great pleasure when I do the best that can to do quality work for other people whether if it is a paying job a volunteer job or working in the church.

RHYTHM

Rhythm is something we all get when we listen to beautiful music. Rhythm is something we get into when we dance to music. Rhythm is something that is for everyone. Rhythm is something that we all need in our lives to take our minds off of our problems. Rhythm is something that always gives us all joy and happiness. Rhythm is something that also give a lot of pleasure in our lives.

ENTHUSIASTIC

Enthusiastic is something that I always feel when I know that I have something to do to help myself and someone else. Enthusiastic is something that I always feel when it comes to preying and worshiping our Lord. Enthusiastic is something that I always feel when I know that I am going to get a honor of a certificate or a wooden plaque for the wonderful work that I always put into everything I do. Enthusiastic is something that I always feel when my editor at Expressions Journal Publishing Company LLC in Milwaukee, Wisconsin always do an excellent job of printing and publishing my books of poetry and essays.

UP AGAINST

Up Against is something that I sometimes come in my everyday life when I have a problem or emergency that arises. Up Against is something that I always need help with by my doctors social workers and specialty healthy care professionals. Up Against sometimes will cause me to worry and panic but I always have my faith in God to help calm me down and get the help that I need. Up Against is will sometimes come my way when another person that I know or a stranger will give me social problems. Up Against is something that with my faith in God and my educational backgrounds will help me on how to solve any problem or crisis that comes my way in everyday living.

AROUND

Around is something that is when someone or thing that is there me. Around is something that has either been around for hundreds or thousands of years or just a few years. Around can be any person place or thing that is lingering around and is bothering people. Around is something that is around the corner or across the street. Around is something that can be something we all love to have around.

ABOUT THE AUTHOR

In my titled Triumphs of Life I did my best to write about the things that reflect our everyday lives. In this book I think that I did an excellent job of writing poems that touch the hearts of all of my readers and those that just scan through this book.

I believe that this book will warm the hearts and souls of everyone that picks up this book to read in their spare time. I believe that I have put forth my best thoughts and writings in this book and I think that my readers will agree.

Rainy Days

BY
DOREENA WILSON

DEDICATION

I dedicate this book to the everyday things that we all face in our everyday lives. I also dedicate this chapter to God because without him I do not think that I would not have been able to come up with the kinds of topics to write about.

FORWARD

I forward this book to all of the people that I see and talk to in my everyday life. I also forward this book to all of the things that I have to do in my everyday life.

FRIENDSHIP IS . . .

Friendship Is having a friend that you can count on. Friendship Is having a friend that you can tell things to without it being spread all over town. Friendship Is having a friend that you can go out to dinner with. Friendship Is having a friend that you can pray with. Friendship Is having a friend that will not turn on you.

THE HOLIDAY SEASON

The Holiday Season is a big celebration of the birth of our Lord Jesus Christ. The Holiday Season is a time of reflecting on all our blessings and gifts. The Holiday Season is a time to give presents in honor of our Lord Jesus Christ. The Holiday Season is a time to enjoy the all of the plentiful harvests that comes from the all of the hard working farmers all across our wonderful country. The Holiday Season is a joyous time of the year.

WHAT PEACE MEANS TO ME

What Peace Means To Me is that God will soon send his precious son Jesus Christ back to end all of the pain, suffering and sin in this world. What Peace Means To Me is that just as the bible says is that all of the saints in their graves will arise first and then all of the living saints will be changed in a moment and will meet up with him. What Peace Means To Me is that well will all see our Lord and Savior just as he is. What Peace Means To Me is that the earth and heavens will all pass away and that will have no more suffering, sickness sin and death.

THE PROMISE

The Promise is something that the our Lord and Savior Jesus Christ has promised in is word that he would come back for his church. The Promise is something that is of love peace and hope. The Promise is something that all of his people have hope in. The Promise is something that will never go away. The Promise is something that all believers have a right and a privilege to go out into this dark and sinful world and preach the word of God to all of the lost souls. The Promise is something that all of God people have comfort and joy knowing that his promise was paid for on the cross.

MY NEW YEARS RESOLUTION

My New Years Resolution is that I will try not to miss so much of the Sunday morning church services at my church that is located just next door to my apartment building. This year I plan on trying to get to get to bed early enough to get up early enough on Sunday mornings to get to church on time every Sunday. I have been going to my Wednesday night Christian Support Group call Living Grace that meets at my church every first and third Wednesday night of the month. I also have been attending Thursday night bible study every week when ever Pastor Paul Bartleme can come to lead bible study.

MY MEDICAL TEST

My Medical Test that I had with my annual mammogram at Aurora Health Care Clinic in Milwaukee, Wisconsin on Thursday, December 20, 2018 was kind of a scary moment for me. My X-Ray Technician Nancy called me the very next morning on Friday, December 21, 2018 at approximately at 9:28AM to let me know that the Radiologist found several very tiny fragments of calcium deposits on my right breast. So she set up an appointment for me to come in on Tuesday, January 8, 2019 9:00AM for a follow-up mammogram so that they can have a further look at my right breast to see if anything was wrong. So on the day of my follow-up I got good news Dr. Christopher J. Zellmer M.D. told me that there was no cancer the three tiny fragments were benign.

BLACK HISTORY MONTH

Black History Month is a month for everyone no matter what ethnic group, race, religion or educational background you come from you all are a part of this important month. I myself as being a black woman am proud of where my people have accomplished over the past 400 years and at the same time I think that all of us are worst off now than we were during the civil rights movement. I am now very troubled with what I see in this era of Black American History. I think that it will continue to only get worst instead of getting better. I am trying to do whatever I can in my own life as a Black Christian Woman to live for our Lord and Savior Jesus Christ and try my best to continue to keep Dr. Martin Luther King Jr.'s legacy alive.

JESUS MAKES ME HAPPY

Jesus Makes Me Happy because I know that his Heavenly Father loved us enough to send down on earth to die for our sins. Jesus Makes Me Happy because I have repented my sins to him for over 32 years. Jesus Makes Me Happy because I know that I will one see him and all his glory in heaven one day. Jesus Makes Me Happy because I know that he is the one who in control of everything in this sinful world. Jesus Makes Me Happy because he is the one who will judge all of us according to our works one day. Jesus Makes Me Happy because I know that he is returning to earth one day and will rule for eternity.

MY JOB INTERVIEW

My Job Interview was for a second shift part-time seasonal position that I applied for at a warehouse company called Scholastic that was listed on one of two job sites that I am currently registered on called indeed.com. My Job Interview was set up in just four days after I applied on line when I received a phone by an employer by the name of Lance. My Job Interview went very well and it was very short and quick when he showed me what the warehouse looked like. My Job Interview did not work well because he told me that there would be a lot of heavy lifting of boxes. My Job Interview ended by Lance saying to me that this job does not look like a fit for you we told each other thank you for coming out to the company and good-bye.

GROCERY SHOPPING

Grocery Shopping is something that I like to do because I like to plan my weekly meals to cook and eat. Grocery Shopping is something that everyone does no matter what walk of life they come from. Grocery Shopping is something that some people do not like to do because they do not either know how plan their weekly meals cook and clean-up. Grocery Shopping is something that they would rather not do because it is easier for them to just go out to and a lot of money to eat at expensive restaurants, fast joints or ordering out for food. Grocery Shopping is good for people to do every week or every month depending on your money situation. Grocery Shopping is gives you a variety of options of all the different foods to eat everyday.

MY BOYFRIEND ALEX

My Boyfriend Alex and I have been together for over 26 years. My Boyfriend Alex and I met at a two-year technical college Milwaukee Area Technical College in Milwaukee, Wisconsin. My Boyfriend Alex and I met when I was serving on one of five student organizations called MATC Downtown Milwaukee Student Senate as a student senate member. My Boyfriend Alex and I met approximately at 12:00 noon on Thursday, October 1, 1992. My Boyfriend Alex and I both from the beginning knew that we would continue to see each other on a regular basis. My Boyfriend Alex and I have been in love with each other every since.

WHAT I LOVE ABOUT LIFE

What I Love About Life is that it is a gift of God. What I Love About Life is that I give all of the praise and worship to our Lord and Savior Jesus Christ. What I Love About Life is that God gives us all a choice to either follow him or not follow him. What I Love About Life is that God has given us his son Jesus on Christmas Day and that is when he gave us a Savior to come and die on the cross for our sins. What I Love About Life is that when we as Christians repented our sins and gave our all to Jesus Christ we will one day see him in all of his glory and majesty.

MY MUSIC CHOICES

My Music Choices that I like to listen to is christian, gospel, classic rock, classic soul ballads, country pop, classical and Broadway. My Music Choices is a variety of seven categories that most people can relate to. My Music Choices is a variety that I grew-up listening to all throughout my life. My Music Choices is something that no one can ever talk me out of listening to. My Music Choices is that I chose when I was a child because that is all of the kind of music that was that beautiful and pleasing to my ears.

BEING SINGLE

Being Single is something that I enjoy and it gives me the freedom to do the things that I want to do. Being Single is something that a lot of people complain about because they always want to know why they are not married yet. Being Single is something that I look at as wonderful. Being Single is something I like because I can get up and go places without anyone hounding me about where I am going. Being Single is that I can plan all of the different kinds of schedules that gives me the freedom to do the all of the things that I need to get done.

COOKING

Cooking is something that I love to plan on doing everyday. Cooking is something that I like because I have a variety of different foods that I love to eat. Cooking is a lot of fun if you know what you are doing in the kitchen. Cooking and planning my menus everyday is a must for me because it gives me an idea of what kinds things to put on my grocery list. Cooking is a wonderful art and anyone can learn how to do it. Cooking is something that I learned how to do when I was in the fourth grade.

THE LETTER

The Letter was written when I put my heart and soul into what I wanted to say. The Letter was written in complete sentences and in complete thought. The Letter was a letter of acknowledgments and congratulations to a friend who has accomplished so much in her life. The Letter was a letter of love and friendship that has endured for many years. The Letter was a letter that I felt that was well accepted.

THE CEREMONY

The Ceremony was a beautiful special occasion that I will never forget. The Ceremony was so wonderful and so much fun I want to celebrate it everyday. The Ceremony will be a time to remember for a lifetime. The Ceremony was a celebration of greatness and accomplishments. The Ceremony a time to reflect and remember all of the hard I put into my education. The Ceremony was joyous time for everyone that attend this special occasion. The Ceremony will not ever be forgotten. The Ceremony is a time that happens every year.

THE MUSIC CONCERT

The Music Concert was a wonderful time for all that attended. The Music Concert will never be forgotten. The Music Concert tickets was very expensive but was well worth it. The Music Concert is something that everyone had a great listening to. The Music Concert had everyone standing up and cheering, dancing and singing along with the musicians and singers that were performing. The Music Concert had everyone on their feet all throughout the show. The Music Concert memories will live on forever.

THE PORTRAIT

The Portrait is something that is so beautiful and wonderful for everyone to look at. The Portrait was painted with mastery and grace. The Portrait was full of life, color and style. The Portrait was painted on a big white cotton fiber canvas. The Portrait was painted in reds, blues, yellows, violates, greens and oranges . The Portrait was a picture of all of the colors of the rainbow and it stood out during the day when the sun shinned. The Portrait was a favorite at the art fair.

THE AWARD SHOW

The Award Show is a show that everyone wants to watch see who will win. The Award Show is an occasion that everyone looks forward to watching every year. The Award Show is an event that everyone that attends gets dressed up in evening gowns and tuxes. The Award Show is an occasion that everyone will be doing their best to win an award. The Award Show is something that is well worth looking forwards to because if you are talented and gifted you have a chance to win an award.

THE PERFECT BIRTHDAY PARTY

The Perfect Birthday Party to me means brain storming what you really want for your party. The Perfect Birthday Party for me means that I would want a buffet style dinner birthday party with backed chicken and gravy, backed glazed ham, red mashed potatoes, cut green beans with onions and mushrooms, soft dinner roles with fresh delicious diabetic bakery and plenty of soft drinks, juices and ice water. The Perfect Birthday Party would also need a live band to perform and a lot of guests and do not forget the big perfect diabetic birthday cake and ice cream to top everything off and tons of presents and money.

MY HIGH SCHOOL CLASS REUNION

My High School Class Reunion was a wonderful time for me to see all of my old high school classmates. My High School Class Reunion had buffet style dinner, a live DJ with a dance floor and a cash bar where you can get all of the free soda you wanted. My High School Class Reunion had some of our old high school teachers that attended our reunion. My High School Class Reunion class president encouraged us to bring in our memorabilia so that everyone can see what you have accomplished since high school. I brought in a typed five page report on what I have accomplished since high school and everyone was very surprised to see me. My High School Class Reunion was held at a large dinner hall in the south side of Milwaukee, Wisconsin called The Carl.

MY ACCOMPLISHMENTS

My Accomplishments are a variety of things that required a lot of hard work that I myself put in volunteering my time and energy with helping others. My Accomplishments was awarded with certificates a wooden placqes. My Accomplishments has been known all throughout my community for my ability to recognize that there was a need to help others in a crisis. My Accomplishments required a lot of other people than myself to get all of the work done that needed to get done. My Accomplishments was volunteering in education, government, church and military.

MISS INDEPENDENT

Miss Independent is what my late Uncle Thomas D. Malone called me all of the time. Miss Independent is what I became when I had to do a lot of soul searching to relearn and rethink about everything that I was doing wrong in my life. Miss Independent took a lot of hard work and a lot of time for me to become the person I am now. Miss Independent is what God has made me to become the woman that has a strong faith in him. Miss Independent is something that everyone that I know admire about me and always look up to for. Miss Independent is me being the person a want to be until my life is over.

MY COLLECTABLES

My Collectales are a collection of a lot of things I love and adore. My Collectibles fits my personality and tells my friends and family what kind of person I am. My Collectables are momentum's that express the kind of good taste I have in what I like. My Collectables consist a collection of stuffed hand made pottery, teddy bears, dolls, stamps, movie videos, music CD's certificates and awards and college degrees.

MY BIG DAY

My Big Day was a day filled with worship and faith. My Big Day was when I gave my life over to the Lord in June of 1976 at the age 19. My Big Day gave me a peace of tranquility that I had never known before. My Big Day was a beautiful hot and sunny day and it was a day that I knew that would lead me to the Lord. My Big Day was a day that I will never forget and it was a day that I will continue to share with everyone I meet for the rest of my life.

THE DAY I GOT BAPTISED

The Day I Got Baptized was a cold and sunny afternoon on February 9, 1997 when I was at the of 40. The Day I Got Baptized will be a day that I will never forget and a day that I will always cherish. The Day I Got Baptized was a day that I decided to die on the cross with our Lord and Savior Jesus Christ and live again. The Day I Got Baptised was a day that their was done in front of a lot of witnesses and it was a day that I washed all of my sins away.

THE CHOIR

The Choir that I heard at the Christmas concert sung so beautifully and wonderful. The Choir that I heard had a harmony of voices that I and everyone there had a great time listening to them sing all of the traditional Christmas Carols that we grew up loving and listening to all of our lives. The Choir was so well trained and did such a magnificent job performing for everyone. The Choir was well dressed and the musicians that accompanied them did such a wonderful job in playing the music to assist the choir with all of the performances that they practiced doing. The Choir performance was well worth my time.

MY DAILY ACTIVITIES

My Daily Activities keeps so busy everyday that I have to plan the night before so that I can fit everything in that needs to get done. My Daily Activities everyday consists of meeting with my social worker, doctors appointments, going to the bank, and grocery shopping, doing chores, laundry, cooking, and taking care of business and making phone calls. My Daily Activities also consists of checking my mail box, email and facebook messages.

LISTENING TO MY RADIO STATION

Listening To My Radio Station consists of listening to my favorite radio station Christian Family Radio coming out of San Diego, California. Listening To My Favorite Radio Station consists of learning that this station has been on the air for over 60 years . Listening To My Radio Station is something that I have been listening to for over three years now. Listening To My Radio Station is something that I enjoy everyday and I love the music, bible teachings and sermons that they broadcast everyday. Listening To My Radio Station helps me to keep in fellowship with God.

LOOKING FOR A JOB

Looking For A Job is what I am doing at the present time. Looking For A Job takes a lot of time, research and patience. Looking For A Job takes a lot of thinking about where your education background and skills lay. Looking For A Job requires a lot of skill. Looking For A Job is not easy to do for most people. Looking For A Job requires you to really think about what you want to do. Looking For A Job requires you to think about what you are really worth salary wise. Looking For A Job requires you to really think about what is the best job that will be right for your education background and job skills.

I THINK THAT WRITING POETRY IS RIGHT FOR ME

I Think That Writing Poetry Is Right For Me because of my strong ability to really think about what I want to write about. I Think That Writing Poetry Is Right For Me because of the wonderful subjects I have been able to write about. I Think That Writing Poetry Is Right For Me because I have really put all of my heart and soul into what to write about. I Think That Writing Poetry I Right For Me because of the all of the wonderful heart felt comments I have received about my poems.

COMMUNICATING WITH OTHERS

Communicating With Others is something that I really enjoy a lot of. Communicating With Others is an excellent way for me to get out of my comfort zone and let other people know what I think and believe. Communicating With Others is something that I think that most people enjoy doing because you can make a lot of new friends that way. Communicating With Others is a good way to practice your ability to get up in front of a group of people and give speech. Communicating With Others is a great outlet for me because I get so wrapped up in my own world.

MY CHILDHOOD EASTER SPEECHES

My Childhood Easter Speeches is something that I looked foreword doing in church with my two younger sisters every year. My Childhood Easter Speeches is something that my mother wanted to pick out a long Easter speech every year after new years. My Childhood Easter Speeches is something that she would gather the three of us up and have read the long poem and we would have fun practicing and learning the words to the speech. My Childhood Easter Speech what called Crucify Him.

EATING OUT

Eating Out is something I enjoy doing very much. Eating Out is a lot of fun for me because there are so many wonderful restaurants for me to eat out at. Eating Out is something that I notice a lot of people doing when I go out to eat. Eating Out can be very expensive if you do it a lot. Eating Out is not something that everyone can afford to do. Eating Out is a way to get out and see the community and meet new people. Eating Out is a way to try new and different menus. Eating Out is a joy for me because I can get away from my everyday schedule.

SAVING FOR RETIREMENT

Saving for Retirement is something that I take seriously. Saving For Retirement is something that everyone who works at a job is doing. Saving For Retirement is something that we all will have to do when we work on an honest job. Saving For Retirement is something that I am looking forwards to when I retire at the age of 67. Saving For Retirement is something that I am happy to do for myself. Saving For Retirement is well worth my time.

CLEANING MY APARTMENT

Cleaning My Apartment is something I take pride in doing when it is in need of a good cleaning. Cleaning My Apartment takes at two hours of my time every week. Cleaning My Apartment is something that everyone in my building does at least once or twice a week. Cleaning My Apartment requires me to also do my laundry once a month. Cleaning My Apartment is something that needs to be done because there is no one else to do it for me. Cleaning My Apartment comes easy for me because I have been doing chores every since the forth grade.

SITTING FOR A PORTRAIT

Sitting For A Portrait is something that everyone enjoys doing. Sitting For A Portrait is a lot of fun to do. Sitting For A Portrait is something that many people look forwards to doing. Sitting For A Portrait takes a lot of skill and patience. Sitting For A Portrait takes only several minutes. Sitting For A Portrait has a lot of different options and styles. Sitting For A Portrait is for anyone who can afford to have picture done.

MY SIXTEENTH BIRTHDAY PARTY

My Sixteenth Birthday Party was something that I can remember just like it was yesterday. My Sixteenth Birthday Party was shared with my two young sister who fraternal twins who was a year younger than I was. My Sixteenth Birthday Party was something that my mother and father wanted to put on for us. My Sixteenth Birthday Party took a lot of planning. My Sixteenth Birthday Party was a blast.

THE FAMILY BACK YARD BARBECUE

The Family Backyard Barbecue was something that my mother and father would plan to put on every summer. The Family Backyard Barbecue was something that we as so many other families around the country would look forwards doing every year. The Family Backyard Barbecue is something that was always fun and exciting. The Family Backyard Barbecue would have a menu of barbecued ribs, chicken, hot dog, polish sausage, potato salad, baked beans, and a very big tub of ice cold sodas and all kinds of deserts. The Family Backyard Barbecue was something that all of our church friends would look forward to coming to enjoy with us.

MY FRIENDS

My Friends are a big blessing to me because we all look out for each other. My Friends comes from ethnic groups, educational backgrounds, and walks of life. My Friends are a big part of my everyday life because I do not get to see my family daily. My Friends and I like to share different kinds of foods with each other. My Friends and I likes to pray for each other. My Friends and I have different problems and situations that we all have to encounter on a day to day basis. My Friends and sometime have disagreements and arguments but in the end we always seem to work it all out. My Friends and I have been through thick and thin in our lives.

MY FAVORITE ENTERTAINMENT

My Favorite Entertainment is listening to christian, gospel, pop and classic rock, disco and soul and R & B music from the 1950's, 1960's, 1970's, 1980's, and early 1990's. My Favorite Entertainment is also watching music concerts, Christmas and Easter specials, and nastsalsha, bible, and history movies and TV shows. My Favorite Entertainment is my very own style and reflects the of entertainment that is all of my own choices.

MY COLLEGE EDUCATION

My College Education was an experience that I will never forget. My College Education was a lot of long hours and hard work. My College Education took a lot out me because I was coming out of ears with writing essays. My College Education required that I had to take four different levels of English writing classes, two different levels of algebra classes and one statistic math class. My College Education also required that I also had to take some vocal, art, ceramic, drawing, theater, and dance and cooking classes. My College Education encouraged me to join five different student organizations.

MY PASTOR AND HIS WIFE

My Pastor And His Wife are both a very big blessing to my church congregation. My Pastor And His Wife are very Godly people. My Pastor And His Wife both have jobs that they work on besides being pastors of my church. My Pastor And His Wife have four children and one grandchild. My Pastor And His Wife have been friends of mine for almost three years now. My Pastor And His Wife and their family are from San Diego, California.

MY PASS TIME HOBBY

My Pass Time Hobby is writing poetry. My Pass Time Hobby is putting things on paper that I think that my readers will enjoy reading about. My Pass Time Hobby is wanting to share what is on my mind and what I like to do. My Pass Time Hobby is hoping that I leave a positive impact on my readers that they will pass the word to all of there friends and families what a great writer I am.

WHAT A BUSY DAY

What A Busy Day I had today. What A Busy Day I had a big day today because I had a dental appointment to get my upper dentures adjusted so that they would no longer hurt my upper gums. What A Busy Day I had today when I had a 1:30PM meeting with my new intake professional Sarah so she could talk with about whether or not if I would be interested in admitted into the CCS Comprehensive Community Services Program that is offered the WHCG Whole Health Clinical Group located in Milwaukee, Wisconsin. What A Busy Day I thought that this program was a great for me.

I AM THE FIRST PERSON IN MY FAMILY TO GRADUATE FROM COLLEGE

I Am The First Person In My Family To Graduate From College because I was encouraged by my parents to go. I Am The First Person In My Family To Graduate From College is something that a lot of other people have done. I Am The First Person In My Family To Graduate From College is something that a lot of people admire me for doing. I Am The First Person In My Family To Graduate From College is something that I myself is excited about. I Am The First Person In My Family To Graduate From College gives me a since of great accomplishments.

MY BLESSED LIFE

My Blessed Life is something that I think that God has given me. My Blessed Life is something that I give God all of the praise and glory for. My Blessed Life is the fact that I had a mother, father and two fraternal twin sisters to grow up with. My Blessed Life is the fact that I had grandparents, aunts, uncles and a host of cousins in my life. My Blessed Life is the fact that I had a christian house to grow up in. My Blessed Life is the fact that I had a normal childhood. My Blessed Life is the fact that I had an excellent education.

A WONDERFUL COUNTRY

A Wonderful Country is the fact that we are all no matter what walk of life we come from we live in a great country. A Wonderful Country is the fact that even though that we had slavery in the south this country has come a long way. A Wonderful Country is the fact this society still has a long way to go for recovery. A Wonderful Country is the that our citizens are all divided we still have a lot in common.

THE FOODS THAT I LOVE TO EAT

The Foods That I Love To Eat is a big variety of different menus. The Foods That I Love To Eat is sometime are the healthiest. The Foods That I Love To Eat is Soul Food, Chinese, Mexican, Italian, German, and American. The Food That I Love To Eat comes from a wide range of different ethnic groups and tastes. The Foods That I Love To Eat takes a lot of planning, time and work to prepare.

I MADE THE NATIONAL DEANS LIST WITH HONORS FOR THE 2004-2005 SCHOOL YEAR

I Made The National Deans List With Honors For The 2004-2005 School Year because when they asked the Dean of Student Affairs James Hill at the University of Wisconsin-Milwaukee to give them a list of great students to enter into the 28th annual year book he told me that my name was one of the students on the that he gave them. I Made The National Deans List With Honors For The 2004-2005 School year because they liked me and because I never had below a 2.5 grade point average. I Made The National Deans List With Honors For The 2004-2005 School Year and I will never forget it.

A GOOD AFTERNOON NAP TIME

A Good Afternoon Nap Time is something that I have to get piratically everyday. A Good Afternoon Nap Time is something that is very much needed for me. A Good Afternoon Nap Time is something that I think that a lot of other people needs as well. A Good Afternoon Nap Time is very much welcomed in my every day life. A Good Afternoon Nap Time is especially needed on the weekends whether if it sunny or cloudy and rainy or a snow blizzard outside.

I LIKE TO TRAVEL

I Like To Travel because I like to see all of the beautiful trees, bushes, flowers, and houses, restaurants, stores, and buildings that is out there. I like To Travel because it also allows me to relax and get away from my everyday schedules and activities. I Like To Travel because I like meet and mingle with new and interesting people from all walks of life. I Like To Travel because I like to see what else is available out there. I Like To Travel because I like to try to cuisine at the different restaurants and eating places. I Like To Travel most of all because I like to collect souvenirs to go with all of my other collectibles.

AWARDS AND HONORS

Awards And Honors are something that is wonderful and exciting to receive for your hard work and efforts. Awards And Honors are a great way for other people who do not know of you and your work to get a chance to see a sample of what you have accomplished in your life. Awards And Honors is well worth the effort because I think that everyone that gets an award and/or honor has done a wonderful job to deserve it.

STAGE PLAYS AND MUSICALS

Stage Plays And Musicals are something that everyone love to see. Stage Plays And Musicals are something that is very entertaining. Stage Plays And Musicals makes people happy. Stage Plays And Musicals are a lot of fun to watch on live stage. Stage Plays And Musicals are very colorful. Stage Plays And Musicals have very beautiful stage settings. Stage Plays And Musicals have very talented actors, dancers and singers. Stage Plays And Musicals are very exciting and dynamic.

I THANK GOD FOR MY BEAUTIFUL GIFT OF WRITING POETRY

I Thank God For My Beautiful Gift Of Writing Poetry because I think that the poets have a great talent to share. I Thank God For my Beautiful Gift Of Writing Poetry because I think that I have something say and I want to share it with others. I Thank God For My Beautiful Gift Of Writing Poetry because of the endless things I can write about. I Thank God For My Beautiful Gift Of Writing Poetry because so many things come to my mind to write about. I Thank God For My Beautiful Gift Of Writing Poetry because of one of my former instructors at Milwaukee Area Technical College encouraged the whole class to write poetry and the first thing I thought about was that now that is something I can do as a talent.

MY ABILITY TO PAY ATTENTION TO DETAILS

My Ability To Pay Attention To Details is something that I noticed that I can do every since I was in the forth grade. My Ability To Pay Attention To Details is something that a lot of my teachers administrators, counselors, doctors, and professors, friends, family and acquaintances have noticed and complimented me on. My Ability To Pay Attention To Details is something that is not always easy to do when you are in a big hurry or under a lot of pressure to get things done on time.

MY GOOD TASTE IN FASHION AND ACCESSORIES

My Good Taste In Fashion And Accessories is something that I think that a lot of people have. My Good Taste In Fashion And Accessories is something that I think that comes easy when you are kind of picky about what you like. My Good Taste In Fashion And Accessories is something that took me a long time to develop. My Good Taste In Fashion And Accessories is something that is not always easy. My Good Taste In Fashion And Accessories is something that has come naturally for me over the years.

MY FRIENDS AND ACQUAINTANCES

My Friends And Acquaintances has changed a lot over the past years. My Friends And Acquaintances that I knew when I was younger has all moved on in life. My Friends And Acquaintances in resent years has not always been very nice to me. My Friends And Acquaintances that I knew for example my high school friends I do get to see and talk to at our high school reunions and on my facebook page. My Friends And Acquaintances that I do have now in my life there are only a hand full of them that are very nice and will treat me out to dinner.

MY ABILITY TO KEEP UP WITH MY FAITH IN GOD

My Ability To Keep Up With My Faith In God will always get through the day. My Ability To Keep Up With My Faith In God will always help me when I am a little depressed and lonely. My Ability To Keep Up With My Faith In God will always help when I have a decision to make in my life. My Ability To Keep Up With My Faith In God will always help when I am worrying about a problem that I am faced with. My Ability To Keep Up With My Faith In God will always help me keep praying and reading my bible.

ABOUT THE AUTHOR

In my book of poems titled Triumphs of Life I think that I have really written my best work yet. I think that in this book the topics that I have been able to come with to write about was very easy for me this time. I think that my readers will be very pleased to read my book because I think that my poems hits home for a lot of people. I have really put forth a lot of thought and know how in the writing of this book.

I am proud of how I am able to write all of the kinds of poems that I have written over the years. I enjoy writing poetry and I hope that my readers will enjoy reading them.

I have a lot to say and I think that what I have to say is very positive and up lifting. I believe that my poems will be well liked by many people.

Starry Nights

BY
DOREENA WILSON

DEDICATION

I dedicate this book to all of the people that is in my life and to all of the things that I have been able to accomplish in my life. I also would like to say thank you to all of the people that have helped me to come up with all of the subjects that I have been able to write about in this book.

FORWARD

I forward this book to my faith in God for without him I would not have been able to write about the subjects that I have been able to write about in this book.

COMMON PEOPLE

Common People all seem to want to be successful. Common People all seem to want to reach for the stars. Common People all want to reach top flight. Common People all want to be loved. Common People all want to be well like. Common People all want to be well respected. Common People all want to be accepted.

HELPLESSNESS

Helplessness is something that none of us wants to feel. Helplessness makes me want to seek help. Helplessness makes me feel anxious. Helplessness makes me want to pray out to God to give me the guidance to make since of it all. Helplessness sometimes gives us grievance. Helplessness is something that a feeling comes when you do not know what else to do.

WHAT I WANT AS A FRIEND

What I Want As A Friend is someone who lifts me up. What I Want As A Friend is someone who is outgoing like myself. What Want As A Friend is someone who has faith in God. What I Want As A Friend is someone who loves to talk. What I Want As A Friend is someone who is not afraid to live their life. What I Want As A Friend is someone is compassionate.

AN OUTSTANDING PERSON

An Outstanding Person is a someone who has overcome obstacles and traumas. An Outstanding Person is someone who has given their life over tot he Lord for their sins. An Outstanding Person is someone who because they were saved can lead a life full of joy, happiness, and hope. An Outstanding Person is someone who has the courage to do anything that everyday life brings their way.

TOGETHERNESS

Togetherness is something I see as people coming together for one cause. Togetherness is something I see as people working together. Togetherness is something I see people praying together. Togetherness is something I see people loving one another. Togetherness is something I see people coming together for righteousness sake.

I HAVE OVERCOME

I Have Overcome my mental illness with a lot of love, support, treatments, hospitalizations, medications and faith in God. I Have Overcome a lot of tough obstacles and failures however I still face obstacles but they are no longer as bad as they were when I first started out on this journey.

FOR THE BEAUTY OF IT ALL

For The Beauty Of It All I have my salvation. For The Beauty Of It All I had my sister who led me there. For The Beauty Of It All I have been forgiven of all my sins and transgressions. For The Beauty Of It All I will see Jesus in all his glory one day. For The Beauty Of It All I will continue to seek Jesus.

MY UNCLE THOMAS

Today I received a phone call from my cousin Kathy that my Uncle Thomas pasted away. I felt very unhappy however we were expecting this for a long time. He had been sick for almost ten years. My Uncle Thomas was a Korean Veteran just like my late father and he was a man of God. I will miss you Uncle Thomas and I love you very much.

UNDERSTANDING

Understanding is something I see as listening and watching. Understanding is something I see ad seeing where another person is coming from listening to what they have to say and seeing where they are in their life. Understanding is also accepting a person fro who they are.

ENCOURAGEMENT

Encouragement is something that I think of as supporting and praying that you will get well soon and come to a full recovery. Encouragement is something that I hope that you will pray for your own recovery and strength in the Lord. Encouragement is something that we all need when we are feeling like there is no light at the end of the tunnel. Encouragement is something that everyone needs when they are feeling down and out on everything that they are trying to work so hard to achieve in their lives.

RESILIENCE

Resilience is something I had when my doctor told me I had stage three kidney disease. Then when he adjusted my medications I went from a stage three kidney disease to a barely stage two kidney disease. Resilience is something that my doctor had just my adjusting my medications. I am now better off than I was a year ago.

TRUTH

Truth is something that I believe will always shine the light on the darkness of life. Truth is something we are all looking for in our selves and in life. Truth is something that will always be the right way for everything we do and say. Truth is something that God teaches in his word. Truth is the only one thing that matters in life. Truth is always appreciated. Truth is something that we all need.

OUR SOLAR SYSTEM

Our Solar System is mighty and beautiful indeed and full of wonder. Our Solar System was created by God and they are here for all of us to enjoy and admire. Our Solar System is here for a reason and that reason is for the earth to survive and thrive. Our Solar System is mighty and beautiful indeed for without it I do not believe we would not be able to survive here on earth.

ATTITUDE

Attitude is everything when you do not have the words to express how you feel about others. Attitude expresses in many ways on how you choose how you feel towards another person whether if you like them or not. Attitude says a lot out loud about how you really feel towards people even when you do not have the words to express how you feel. Attitude can either hurt or make someone happy.

SELF CONFIDENCE

Self Confidence is something that I have achieved when I stepped out of my comfort zone and attended and graduated from the University of Wisconsin-Milwaukee after I had just finished Milwaukee Area Technical College. Self Confidence in myself rose from a 5 to an 8 it took me 17 years to graduate form UWM with a BS Degree in Educational Studies when it only took eight-years and six weeks to graduate from MATC.

FEAR

Fear is something we feel when are afraid that something is about to go wrong. Fear is something that is a part of everyday life. Fear is something that we do not like to feel even if we know that God is near bye and in control of our lives. Fear is something that we feel because we may see or hear about something dangerous happening. Fear is something that brings us all together to fight against the danger that we feel, see or hear that is about to take place. Fear is something that we cannot avoid because it a part of human nature.

EVERYDAY LIFE

Everyday Life is getting up every morning and getting ready to go to school, work or a volunteer job. Everyday Life is after finishing up a very busy day running errands to the bank, store or a restaurant preparing your evening meal and then getting ready to do all of the schedule all over again the next day. Everyday Life is a never ending process and you have the willpower to keep up with it. Everyday Life is something that we all have to face no matter what walk of life we come from.

NATURE

Nature is something that is beautiful to look at no matter if you are into it or not. Nature is something that is a part of our world that will never die. Nature is a part of all of us. Nature is something for all of us to enjoy. Nature is something we all can admire both young and old. Nature is something that God created for without nature we would not be able to survive.

WHAT HIGHLAND COMMONS MEANS TO ME

What Highland Commons Means To Me is that it is a lean and safe place to live. What Highland Commons Means To Me is that it is a brand new apartment building. What Highland Commons Means To Me is that all of the residents look out for each other. What Highland Commons Means To Me is that there is staff and a coordinator here to talk to seven days a week.

EMOTIONS

Emotions is something that we cannot escape. Emotions can be fear. Emotions can be love. Emotions can be happiness. Emotions can be sadness. Emotions can be anger. Emotions can be frustrations. Emotions can be anything that the outside world can cause you to feel. Emotions is something that is a part of life that we cannot avoid. Emotions can make life easy. Emotions can make life hard. Emotions is something that we cannot live without.

MY AFFIRMATIONS

My Affirmations is my faith in God that gets me through the each and everyday of the week. My faith is something that I take seriously and that is a positive thing for me. My Affirmations in my faith up lifts me and I am always sharing my faith with other people. My Affirmations in my faith in God is something that I am glad that I have in my life and in everyday and everything that I do.

THE FALL TIME

The Fall Time makes me feel like sleeping on a cool cloudy rainy days of autumn. The Fall Time is a time when all of the leaves change on trees and turn into different colors like red, orange an yellow. The Fall Time reminds of a time of when the whether turns cool and some days are still worm and sunny. The Fall Time reminds me of all of the harvests of the farms and vegetable gardens that have grown throughout the summer months. The Fall Time reminds me of the football season that have just begun.

THINGS THAT MAKES ME SMILE

Things That Makes Me Smile is someone who is saying funny things. Things That Makes Me Smile is when someone tells me something good. Things That Makes Me Smile is when I hear good news about someone going out of their way to make a difference. Things That Makes Me Smile is when the sun shines outside. Things That Makes Me Smile is when someone gives me a good compliment.

THINGS THAT SCARE US

Things That Scare Us can be many things. Things That Scare Us are some things like bugs crawling all on your legs and arms. Things That Scare Us can be something that the doctor has told us something about our health. Things That Scare Us can be a fear of heights. Things That Scare Us can be fears of the dark. Things That Scare Us can be hearing about someone else getting a serious illness.

THE JOURNEY

The Journey is my faith in God and trying to please only him. The Journey is some that all of us is passing through. The Journey is filled with trials and tribulations. The Journey is filled with love, joy, and happiness. The Journey is filled with thanksgiving. The Journey is having a personal relationship with the Lord. The Journey is praise worship and song. The Journey is giving up everything to the Lord. The Journey is building your foundation on the rock. The Journey is leaning and trusting in the Lord completely.

IF I COULD BE A SUPERHERO

If I Could Be A Superhero I would speak out against all of the injustices in the world. If I Could Be A Superhero I would try to help all of the little children living in poverty. If I Could Be A Superhero I would feed the hungry. If I Could Be A Superhero try to help those that are falsely accused of wrong doing. If I Could Be A Superhero I would help those that cannot help themselves. If I could Be A Superhero I would try to console all of the people that are hurting. If I Could Be A Superhero I would try to visit all of the prisoners that are wrongfully locked up.

GRATITUDE

Gratitude is something that I am grateful for my salvation. Gratitude is something that I am grateful for my excellent health and sound mind. Gratitude is something that I am grateful for my doctors, nurses, social workers, peer specialists, and specialty doctors that all take care of me. Gratitude is something that I am grateful for my education. Gratitude is something that I am grateful for my teachers, professors, instructors, counselors, advisers, tutors, and staff for helping me to reach my goals.

MIRACLES

Miracles are something that is a gift from God. Miracles is the gift of the birth of Christ that was born on Christmas day. Miracles are something that God gives when we wake up each and every morning. Miracles are something when we become a blessing to others. Miracles is something that we have when the doctor says that are have excellent health. Miracles is something that God gives us when we do for ourselves and help others along the way. Miracles is something that we have we have love. Miracles is something that we have when we have family and friends. Miracles is something that we have when we have finances.

BEING SUCCESSFUL

Being Successful depends on each persons perspective. Being Successful takes hard work. Being Successful takes dedication. Being Successful takes persistence. Being Successful is something that everyone wants to be. Being Successful is something that I have achieved in my lifetime. Being Successful is something that everyone wants to achieve. Being Successful is not hard to achieve if you have the right support. Being Successful is something that is wonderful.

CHRISTMAS BLESSINGS

Christmas Blessings is having your right mind and health. Christmas Blessings is having a place to live, food to eat, and clothes to wear on your back. Christmas Blessings is having your family and friends. Christmas Blessings is having my salvation Christmas Blessings is living in a country where we can worship God openly and freely. Christmas Blessings is being able to living in a society where we can just be who we are. Christmas Blessings is a blessing to be alive. Christmas Blessings is blessing that we can give thanks to God for sending is only son Jesus down to die for all of our sins. Christmas Blessings is a time to renew our faith in God.

MY PURPOSE

My Purpose is to serve God and to inspire others to do the same. My Purpose is to tell others about Jesus. My Purpose is to help to teach other how we should treat others the way we want to be treated. My Purpose is to live the way the Lord teaches us to live in front of other so that they can follow along. My Purpose is to love my enemies. My Purpose is is to not take favoritism among others. My Purpose is to serve.

A NEW DAY

A New Day has arrived for me today. A New Day is starting something new. A New Day is going out for my news job interview. A New Day is using the education that worked so hard to get. A New Day has come for me to start my new career. A New Day is here for me to grab. A New Day is here for us all. A New Day is here for us to all enjoy the moment. A New Day is here for us to make the most of it all.

WORDS UNSAID

Words Unsaid are words that we do not express. Words Unsaid is better off when we do not know what a person is like. Words Unsaid is something we all have. Words Unsaid is something we can express at a better time when the tie is right. Words Unsaid are words that we also do not know how, when, and where we can say them. Words Unsaid can be left off for the time being. Words Unsaid is better off when we should just listen.

WHAT LOVE MEANS TO ME

What Love Means To Me is to be together with my boyfriend Alex. What Love Means To Me is to spend time with my family. What Love Means To Me is to be with my friends. What Love Means To Me is give time to the Lord. What Love Means To Me is to be with my church family. What Love Means To Me is to volunteer my time at the VA hospital. What Love Means to Me is to spend time reading my bible. What Love Means To Me is to treat others the way you want to be treated. What Love Means To Me is to love others.

DEAR MARGRET

Dear Margret I will miss you immensely. I will laughing at your jokes. I will seeing you downstairs in the community dinning room and the front lobby. I will miss talking with you. I will miss going up stairs and knocking on your apartment door seeing asking you how are you doing today. I will miss you talking about your family. I will miss hearing your voice and laughter. And most of all I will miss watching and seeing you cheer and yell Hooray for our home teams. Goodbye and rest in peace Dear Margret.

RAINBOWS OF THE MIND

Rainbows Of The Mind reminds me of all the beautiful different races of people in our world. Rainbows Of The Mind reminds me of all the beautiful colors of nature. Rainbows Of The Mind reminds me of all the wonderful blessings that God gives everyday. Rainbows Of The Mind reminds me of all the different species of animals, birds, and creeping bugs that is in our world. Rainbows Of The Mind reminds me that we are all Gods creatures.

SUNSHINE AND THE HORIZON

Sunshine And The Horizon is something the minds me of when the sun rises early in the morning and when the sun sets late in the evening. Sunshine And The Horizon are two things that coincides just perfectly. Sunshine And The Horizon also reminds me how the sun shines so brightly during the day and how the darkness is so dark at night.

WHAT JOY MEANS TO ME

What Joy Means To Me is that the Lord blesses all of us everyday with good health, peace and prosperity. What Joy Means To Me is that we are all God's creatures. What Joy Means To Me is that God sits on the throne and he is in control of everything. What Joy Means To Me is that I thank God for my salvation all the time.

SOMETHING UNBELIEVABLE

Something Unbelievable is that I never thought that I would be able to write poetry as well as I do. Something Unbelievable is something that I never thought I would have all of the wonderful readers reading my poetry. Something Unbelievable something that I never thought that I would ever be a published author. Something Unbelievable is that I never thought I would ever have a Hollywood record company record my one of my poems to Gospel music.

FORGIVE AND FORGET

Forgive And Forget are two things that I am always able to do if the person and people are sincere when they ask for forgiveness. Forgive And Forget is also something that God will do if we are sincere when we ask him for forgiveness. Forgive And Forget is not something that we should play with. Forgive And Forget is some we should all strive to do even when we have been wrongfully done for spite. Forgive And Forget is also something we should do because our Heavenly Father requires us to do so and when we do he will also Forgive And Forget our wrong doing when we ask him for to forgive us for our trespasses.

LISTENING

Listening is something we all do when we want to learn something about a person, place or thing. Listening is something that we should not take very lightly. Listening is something that is very important in everyday life. Listening is something that is required when we are in church. Listening is something that we is required when we are in a class school or college. Listening is something that is required when we are in a job interview. Listening is something that we do when we are watching the news on TV or hearing it on the radio. Listening is something that is a part of every aspect of our lives.

AMBITION

Ambition is something that I have a lot of in my everyday life. Ambition is my faith in God. Ambition is my ability to have the faith to go out and earn my two year and four year degrees. Ambition is me having the faith in God to go out and get a job. Ambition is something that we all have even when we feel like we cannot make it from day to day.

THE QUEEN OF SOUL

The Queen Of Soul was the first the female singer that I have ever heard of when I was just five years old. The Queen Of Soul had a voice that I will never forget. The Queen Of Soul looked like the beautiful women that I dreamed she would look like when I saw the cover of her first album. The Queen Of Soul sung like she was singing her heart out when she recorded her ever famous gospel albums. The queen Of Soul never did anything out of the ordinary. The Queen Of Soul was very positive figure in our ever troubled American Society. The Queen Of Soul will never be forgotten. The Queen Of Soul will highly missed by all of fans all over the world. The Queen Of Soul was none other than Aretha Franklin.

WONDERFUL

Wonderful is something that we all think of a something that great. Wonderful is something that we say to someone that has gone out of their way to help another person. Wonderful is something that we all think of when we see that someone is doing a great job in school or college. Wonderful is something that we all think of when we see someone giving to charity or church. Wonderful is something we all think of when we see someone an exceptional job in their chosen career or job title. Wonderful is something that we all think of when we see someone going out of their comfort zone and going into the peace cores or into missionary work. Wonderful is also something we all think of when we see a young or more mature person joining the military to serve our great country.

HEAVENLY

Heavenly is the first thing that we think of when we see a person giving their life over to the Lord. Heavenly is the first thing that we all think when we see a group of doctors healing a sick person. Heavenly is the first thing we all think of when we see that someone has been healed by God. Heavenly is the first thing that we all think of when we see someone who is mentally or physically handicapped overcoming all odds.

TRAGEDY AND TRIUMPH

Tragedy And Triumph is something that I felt when I lost my father. Tragedy And Triumph is something that I had to get therapy for to get over the deep depression that I felt over the death of my father. Tragedy And Triumph is something that I than God for helping me to get over all of the very deep depression and hurt that I felt during that terrible time in my life.

BLESSINGS

Blessings is a gift from God. Blessings is a joy for all of us to have. Blessings is a wonderful gift from God. Blessings is a beautiful gift from God. Blessings is a great gift from God. Blessings is gift of God. Blessings is a gift of love from God. Blessings is the most wonderful gift that God can give us. But the biggest Blessing that God has ever given us is his son Jesus who died on the cross for all of our sins.

DR. MARTIN LUTHER KING, JR.

Dr. Martin Luther King, Jr. was a great man. Dr. Martin Luther King, Jr. did a great job. Dr. Martin Luther King, Jr. a man of God. Dr. Martin Luther King, Jr. was a great speaker. Dr. Martin Luther King, Jr. was a great leader. Dr. Martin Luther King, Jr. for everybody. Dr. Martin Luther King, Jr. Dr. Martin Luther King, Jr. was a fearless leader. Dr. Martin Luther King, Jr. was wonderful and great leader of all of his people that will always live on forever in our hearts and minds.

EXCELLENT HEALTH

Excellent Health is something the Lord has blessed me with. Excellent Health is something that was achieved by me and my doctors. Excellent Health is something that was achieved by me following all of my doctors orders. Excellent Health is something that was achieved by me taking all of my medications as prescribed by my doctors. Excellent Health is something that was achieved by met attending all of my scheduled doctors appointments, labs and X-Ray and all of my other medical treatment appointments that was scheduled by my doctors.

LOVE SONGS

Love Songs is something that everyone loves to write about. Love Songs is something that everyone loves to sing to. Love Songs is something that everyone loves to listen to. Love Songs is something that all of the radio stations like to play over the air waves. Love Songs is something that everyone even babies, children and teenagers can relate to. Love Songs is something that has been around every since the beginning of time and it will be around forever more.

A PERFECT WORLD

A Perfect World is a world where everyone treats others as they would like to be treated. A Perfect World is a world where there is very little crime. A Perfect World is a world where we did not do not have so much war fare. A Perfect World is a world where we do not have a lot of conflicts. A Perfect World is a world where we do not have so many misunderstandings. A Perfect World is a world where everyone is just getting along together and treating one another with love and respect.

CHARITY

Charity is a gift that I give to my church when I give my tithes every Sunday morning. Charity is a gift that I give when I donate food to feed the hungry. Charity is a gift that I give when I donate clothes, books and stuffed animals to the Salvation Army. Charity is a gift when I give money to the charity of my choice. Charity is a gift when I donate my time to volunteer for a church, VA or political party. Charity is a gift when I give a gift of love and passion to a friend in need.

THE GOOD LIFE

The Good Life is a life that the Lord has blessed me with. The Good Life is a life filled with an excellent health and sound mind. The Good Life is a life filled with the gift of giving back to others. The Good Life is a life that is filled with serving the Lord in many ways. The Good Life is a life of worshiping and loving the Lord with all my might. The Good Life is a life of the blessing of writing poetry so that others can read my work and enjoy it. The Good Life is a life filled with all the things that have ever dreamed of.

THANKS

Thanks for all of the wonderful blessing that you have blessed me with Lord. Thanks for the family, friends and acquaintances that you have put in my life. Thanks for my two year and four year degrees. Thanks for my job and finances. Thanks for the wonderful things that you have allowed me a accomplish in my life. Thanks for waking me up every morning. Thanks for watching over all of us morning, noon and night. Thanks for sending your precious son Jesus down to die for all of our sins.

HOW BRIGHT IT IS

How Bright It Is that the sun shines so bright in the sky. How Bright It Is that you are in my life. How Bright It Is that I have lived to see another day. How Bright It Is that I can get all of the things that needs be done everyday. How Bright It Is that I have the right to write poetry. How Bright It Is that I have this wonderful gift of writing poetry. How Bright It Is that I have a wonderful audience to read my writings. How Bright It Is that I had a former instructor at Milwaukee Area Technical College named Mrs. Mary Louise Stebbens who encouraged me to write poetry.

ONE MORNING

One Morning I woke up and the sun was shining so brightly that I just could not wait to get up and go outside. One Morning I was able to get great news about my excellent health. One Morning it was so hot outside that everybody had to stay indoors and turn their air conditioners. One Morning I my math instructor Mr. Josh Jasuski told me that I passed my statistics class at UWM. On Morning I had a job interview at Horus Mann Elementary School that went so well that the Principal Mr. Jeff Thompson told me that I was hired. One Morning I went to work and had a wonderful day on my first day on the job.

THIS MOMENT

This Moment I have a wonderful idea on how to write this poem. This Moment I had the best time of my life. This Moment I had a nice conversation with my certified peer specialist. This Moment I have a lot of great things going on in my life. This Moment I am very happy. This Moment I feel like there is going to something good that is going to happen. This Moment my life is in excellent shape. This Moment I have a great relationship with my family, friends and acquaintances.

HOW TO LISTEN

How To Listen is something that takes a lot of practice. How To Listen is something that takes a lot of patience. How To Listen is something that is not easy to do. How To Listen is something that a lot of people have trouble doing. How To Listen is something that a lot of people know how to do. How To Listen is something that I have myself sometimes have trouble doing. How To Listen is something that I would say that I am good at doing for most of the time. How To Listen is something is something that I am better doing when I am in a class, lecture or church. How To Listen is something that I need to work on when it comes to talking to my friends on the telephone. How To Listen is something that we all need learn more about.

THE END AND THE BEGINNING

The End And The Beginning is something that goes together very well. The End And The Beginning is something that we all have been taught in school from our young childhood years. The End And The Beginning is something that we can not do without. The End And The Beginning is something that comes naturally. The End And The Beginning is something that tells a story whether if it true or fiction. The End And The Beginning is a part of our everyday lives.

GOD SAYS YES TO ME

God Says Yes To Me not because of what I have done but because of what he has done for me. God Says Yes To Me because I know that I do not deserve his precious grace but because he loves me. God Says Yes To Me because I have given my all to him. God Says Yes To Me because he is our creator. God Says Yes To Me because he knows that without him I would not exist.

MY FATHERS HATS

My Fathers Hats is something that he had a lot of. My Fathers Hats is something that he worked very hard to achieve in his life. My Fathers Hats is something that he wore with pride. My Fathers Hats is something that he did not take for granted. My Fathers Hats is something that he wore with respect. My Fathers Hats is something that I will always remember him for.

KNOWLEDGE

Knowledge is something that all a lot of because of our educational backgrounds. Knowledge is something that all of us can identify with. Knowledge is something that comes naturally. Knowledge is something that we all need in our everyday lives. Knowledge is something that we share with one another. Knowledge is something that we have gotten from our parents. Knowledge is something that we all have gotten from school. Knowledge is something that we all have gotten from colleges and universities. Knowledge is something that we have gotten from the word of God.

ABOUT THE AUTHOR

In my book titled Triumphs of Life I did my best to write about the things that were close to my heart. I am very happy about the kinds of poems that I have been able to write about in this book. I think that my readers will agree with me about that. I am also excited about what the critics will say about the style of my poetry writing. I think that I did my best to reach readers in a way that I would have liked to be reached out to.

I am blessed by God with this wonderful gift of writing poetry and I think that both my readers and critics will all agree. I am pleased that I was able to come up with all of the beautiful subjects to write about in this book. I hope that everyone who reads this book will find the enjoyment in reading this book as well as it was an enjoyment for me to write this book. To everyone who buys my book titled Triumphs of Life I say thank you and God bless you all.

www.ingramcontent.com/pod-product-compliance
Lightning Source LLC
LaVergne TN
LVHW042245070526
838201LV00088B/28